ABC disAbilities

Handicapped No More

Written by Mary Kaluza-Maxson
Illustrated by Sarah Gledhill

atmosphere press

This book is dedicated to my mother, Marge Kaluza, who improved the lives and status of disabled people here in the U.S. and abroad.

This book is also dedicated to my brother, Thomas James Kaluza, who overcame two profound disabilities to succeed in work and life.

Disabled doesn't have to mean without talent. Work hard, try new things, do your best, and always pursue your dreams. Overcome your obstacles and you can succeed. It is ok for anyone to look, act, or think differently than their family, friends, or peers. According to the U.S. Census Bureau data from 2021, the U.S. has over 42 million people with disabilities, 13%.

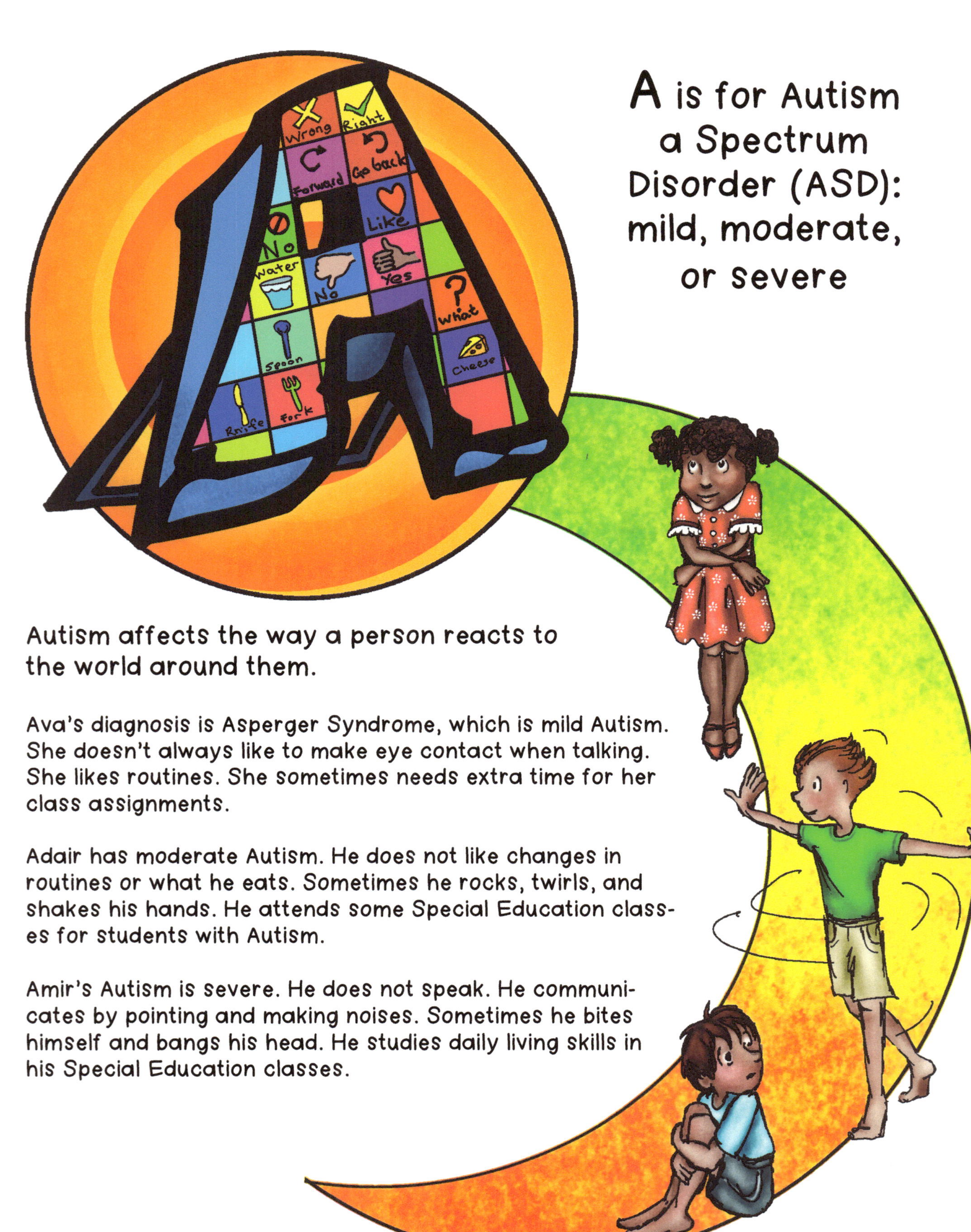

A is for Autism a Spectrum Disorder (ASD): mild, moderate, or severe

Autism affects the way a person reacts to the world around them.

Ava's diagnosis is Asperger Syndrome, which is mild Autism. She doesn't always like to make eye contact when talking. She likes routines. She sometimes needs extra time for her class assignments.

Adair has moderate Autism. He does not like changes in routines or what he eats. Sometimes he rocks, twirls, and shakes his hands. He attends some Special Education classes for students with Autism.

Amir's Autism is severe. He does not speak. He communicates by pointing and making noises. Sometimes he bites himself and bangs his head. He studies daily living skills in his Special Education classes.

B is for Braille

Beryl is legally Blind, she cannot see. She reads words, sentences, paragraphs, and stories through her fingertips. Braille uses patterns of raised dots that represent the letters of the alphabet. Braille is used in books, in the community, and in elevators, at train stations, and in other important areas for instructions and directions. Beryl learned to move through her community with the help of an orientation and mobility teacher.

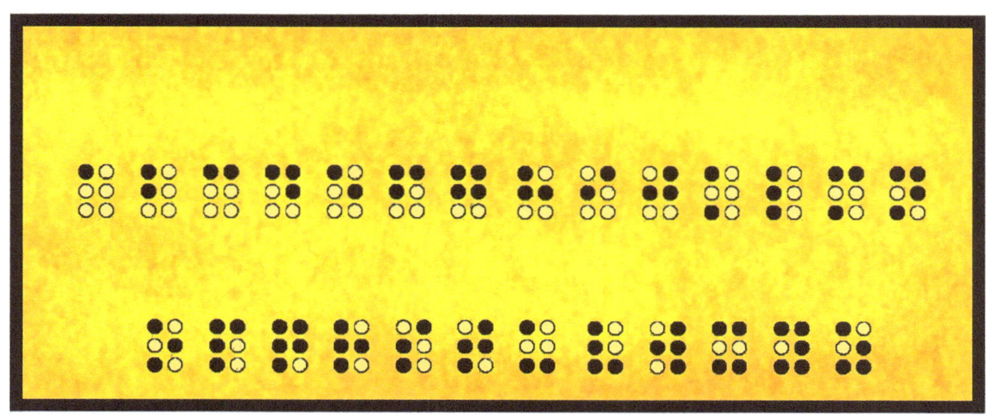

C is for Canine Service Dogs

There are medical search and rescue dogs, military dogs, and police canine units, as well as many other types of service dogs. They support their owners who have physical, emotional, or intellectual disabilities.

Clementine is a seeing eye dog. She is trained to help her blind owner navigate through the community. Clementine sees what her owner cannot see.

Clyde is a therapy dog. His job is to comfort people when they have stress.

Coco is an emotional support dog. She goes with her owner everywhere to keep him or her calm during daily activities.

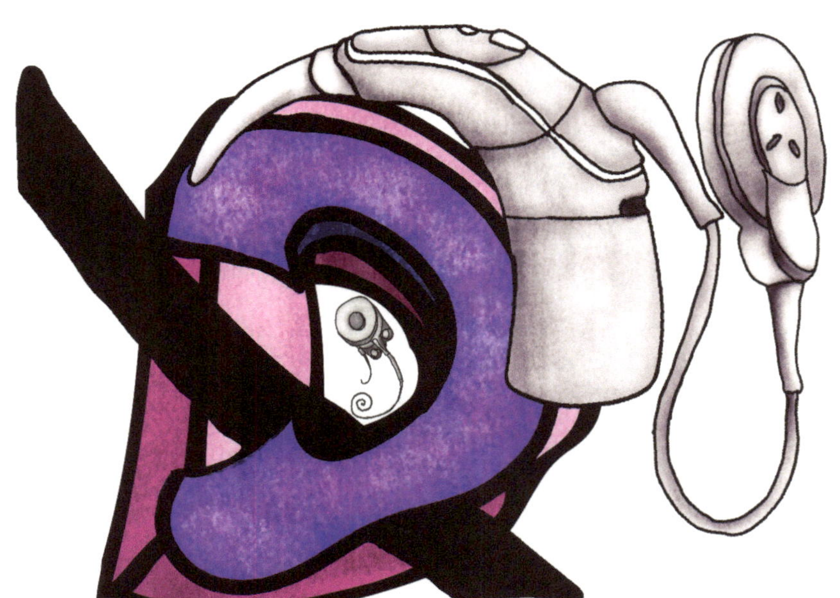

D is for Deaf

Some kids are Deaf or Hard of Hearing in one or both ears. Hearing aids amplify sound and can be helpful. Deaf people often communicate with American Sign Language (ASL), which uses hand movements and finger spelling.

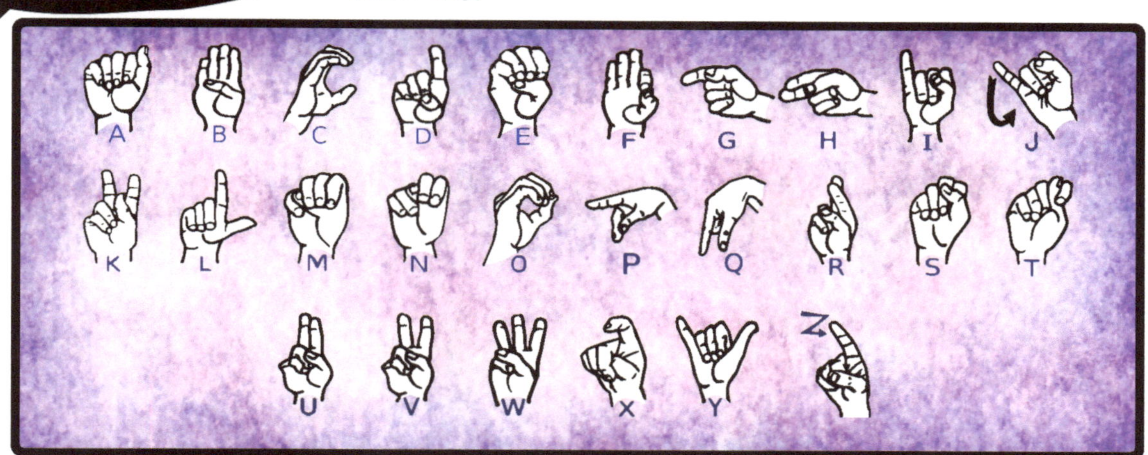

Sign Language interpreters are sometimes used during public events, on TV, or in schools, to help translate spoken words into sign language, for the deaf community.

Hellen Keller was a historic leader who changed the way people think about disabilities. She was Deaf and Blind but was able to overcome the limited expectations people put on her. She was the first Deaf and Blind person in the U.S. to earn a bachelor's degree, and she wrote several books, essays, and gave speeches around the world.

E is for Emotional Disturbance

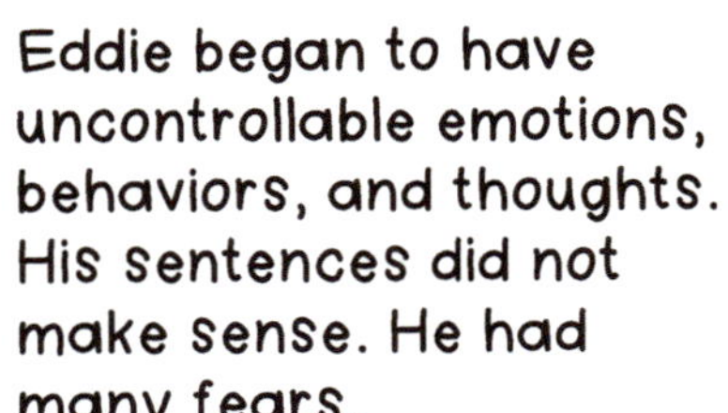

Eddie began to have uncontrollable emotions, behaviors, and thoughts. His sentences did not make sense. He had many fears.

He lost his friends and stopped learning. Eddie's teachers, medical experts, and his family got him academic tutoring and emotional support to help him get along with his classmates, the school staff, his family and people in the community.

F.A.P.E. is an offer you can refuse or accept. It guarantees that all kids with disabilities can attend public school in all fifty states. Some students with disabilities stay in school until they are 22 years old.

G is for Genetics

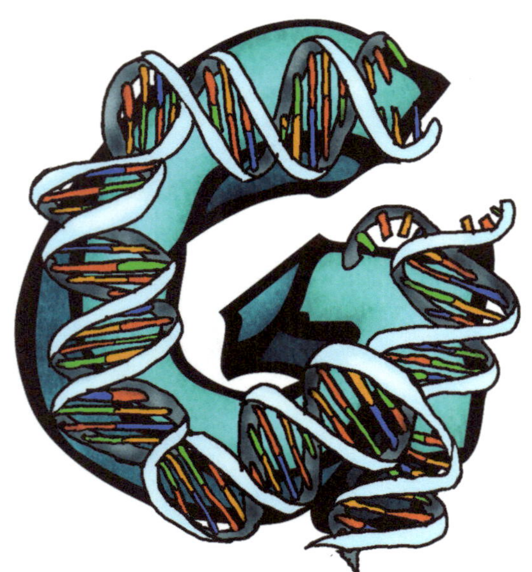

Ginny, Guo, and Guillermo all have genetic diseases. They are sometimes known as birth defects. Babies can inherit extra, deformed, or missing genes on their chromosomes from their parents and grandparents.

Ginny was born with Sickle Cell Anemia, a blood disorder which often affects people of African heritage.

Guillermo was born with Osteogenesis Imperfecta. This is sometimes called Brittle Bone Disease. This is a physical disability that is genetic, where his bones are fragile and easily broken.

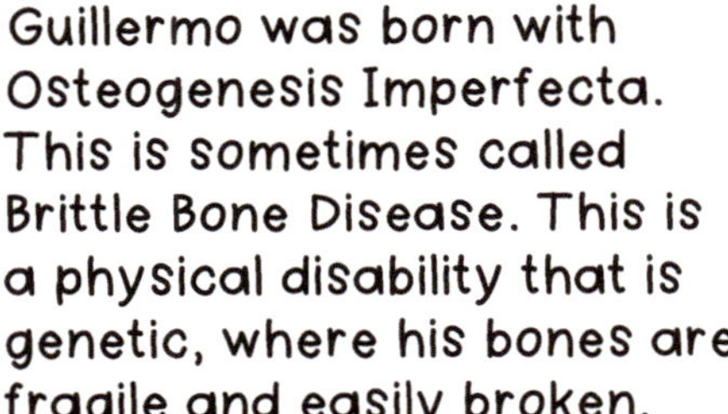

Guo has Muscular Dystrophy. As he gets older, his muscles will become weak making it harder for him to stand and walk on his own. He will need support with his mobility, such as a walker or a wheelchair.

It's good to remember that many diseases are rare and do not happen frequently. Some diseases can cause disabilities but most do not.

H is for Handicapped No More

Many, many years ago someone who was disabled could only beg for money to live. The word "handicap" came from 'cap-in-hand', the image of a person holding an outstretched cap in their hand, begging for money. However, this is a tall tale. The origin of 'cap-in-hand' is actually from an old English trading game.

Handicapped meant low expectations, more restrictions, with little success.

Disabled is a better word that means higher expectations, less restrictions, and greater success.

I is for I.E.P.

An Individual Education Plan is a Federal document in all 50 states for students age 3 to 22 years old, who qualify for services to help them through school. Some students only need extra time for homework and test taking, or for a front row desk. These are accommodations. Other students may need specially designed lessons, smaller classes, and extra academic help in Special Education classes (modifications).

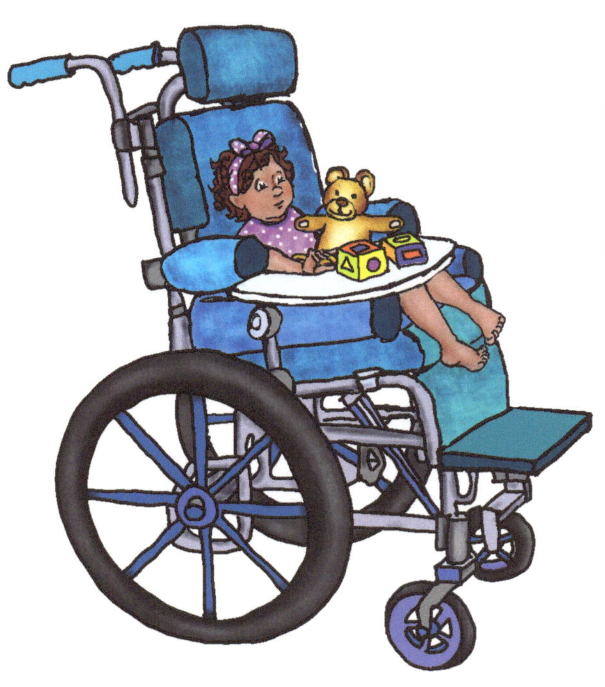

Jasmine is only 3 years old and seems delayed in her physical and intellectual growth.

She points and makes sounds to communicate. She is not able to walk or talk yet.

She is Developmentally Delayed and will be closely watched for any changes.

After age 4, Jasmine could receive Special Ed. services under a new eligibility called Multiple Disabilities Ortho-pedic (MDO).

Kiren was born with Down's Syndrome. He has an Intellectual Disability (ID).

He is a Special Olympic athlete and belongs to the Best Buddies Club where he has disabled and non-disabled friends, and he participates in many activities at his school. For Kiren and others, when they get older, there are many opportunities to work and succeed in their communities.

L is for Laws

Laws protect the rights of disabled people and are passed by Federal legislation.

Some of these laws are: Brown vs The Board of Education, Public Law 94-142, Americans with Disabilities Act (ADA), Individuals with Disabilities Education Act (IDEA), and Rehabilitation Act of 1973, which includes Section 504 Plans for students who need accommodations but can succeed in general education.

Leon is Levi's older brother. Leon has a Specific Learning Disability (SLD). He does not process language like his peers. Learning disabilities can sometimes be inherited. Levi could have learning difficulties as well. He is monitored at school.

Misha moves about quickly, and sometimes pops wheelies in her manual wheelchair. Her neighborhood has accessible curbs, ramps, and buildings with elevators. Her family has a disabled parking pass to use in disabled parking spaces.

No two brains think alike. The word "Neurodivergent" comes from "Neurodiversity", a sociological term that points out that everybody's brain develops in their own individual way. Neurodivergence can be associated with disorders, such as Autism, ADHD, Dyslexia, and many more.

Olivia and Otto are twins. Olivia is unsteady when walking and unbalanced from Cerebral Palsy, a physical disability. She uses crutches when walking. She has an Orthopedic Impairment (OI).

A doctor tested Otto for Attention Deficit Disorder, which is an Other Health Impairment (OHI) disability. It is causing him to lose focus and to be easily side tracked in class. Both have an IEP in school.

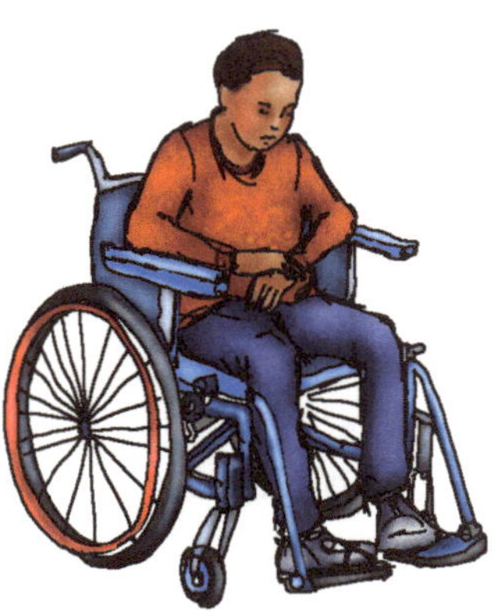

P is for
Professional Experts

Professional Experts have specific skills to help people with disabilities access their education and their community.

Pierre, was a natural athlete, healthy, and an A student in school. After a car accident, Pierre had serious injuries. In the hospital, his medical team included doctors, nurses, occupational, physical, psychological, and speech therapists. They worked with him to speak, walk, and understand his emotions again.

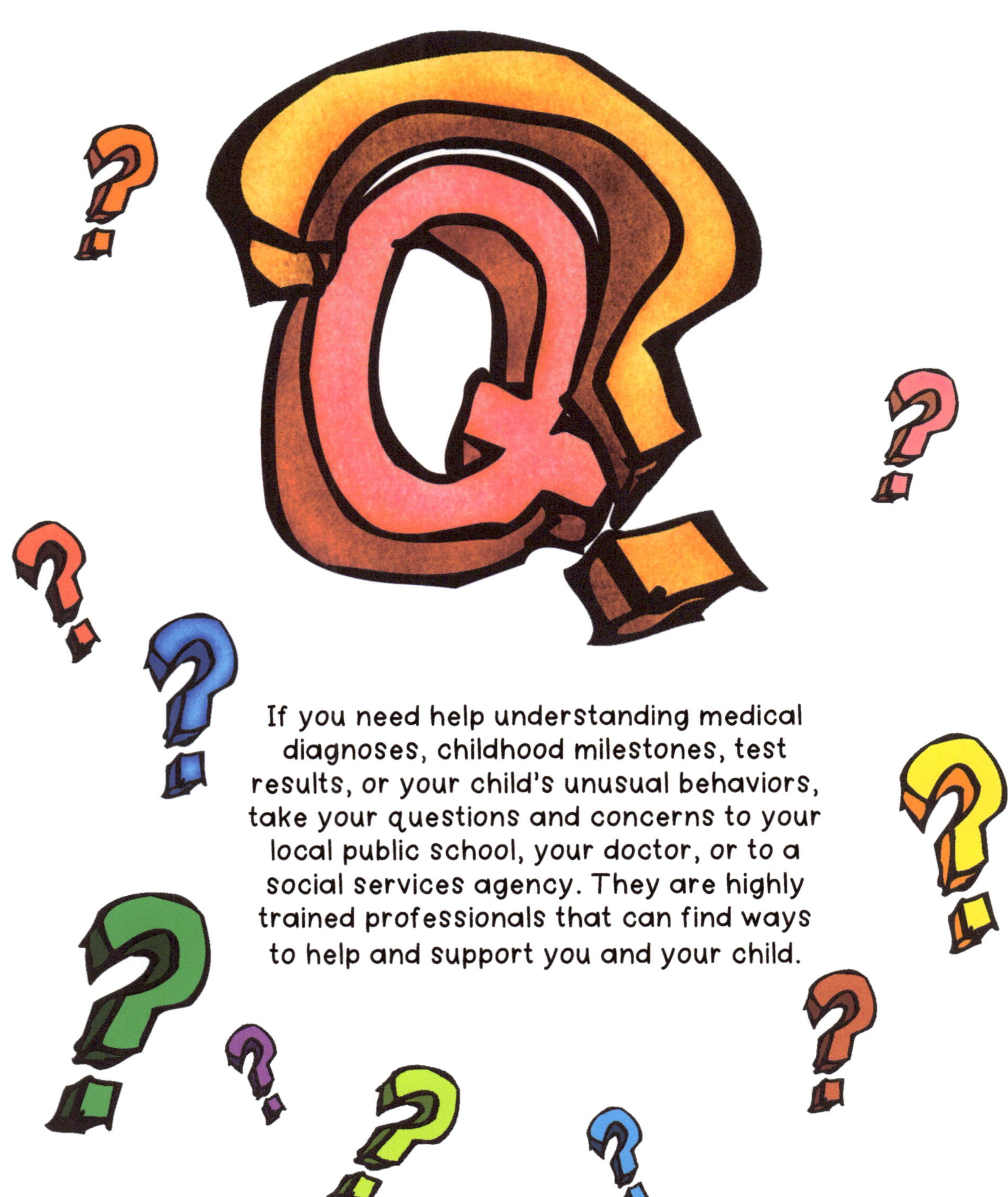

Q is Questions for parents

If you need help understanding medical diagnoses, childhood milestones, test results, or your child's unusual behaviors, take your questions and concerns to your local public school, your doctor, or to a social services agency. They are highly trained professionals that can find ways to help and support you and your child.

R is for

Recreation

There are many exciting
and fun activities designed
for the Disabled.
Here are a few suggestions:

Special Olympics
Camps for Disabled
Deaf Theatre
Adapted playgrounds
Blind skiing
Autism: A Night at
the Theatre

Best Buddies
Equine Therapy
Abilities Expo
Wheelchair sports
Surfing lessons for kids
with Autism

S is for Speech and Language Impairment

Susan sees a speech therapist to learn strategies to reduce her stuttering and speech hesitations. She has a Speech and Language Impairment (SLI).

T is for Traumatic Brain Injury

Trevor was severely shaken as a baby. Tilly fell down a hillside. Travis was in an accident on his bike. All three have suffered a Traumatic Brain Injury (TBI), which is caused by an external or physical force.

This can affect learning, behavior, and decision making. It can also affect thinking, walking, and talking.

U is for Universal Technology

Cell phones, computers, tablets, watches, and TVs are programmed to help the disabled with louder sound, large fonts, text to speech, closed captioning, and location trackers.

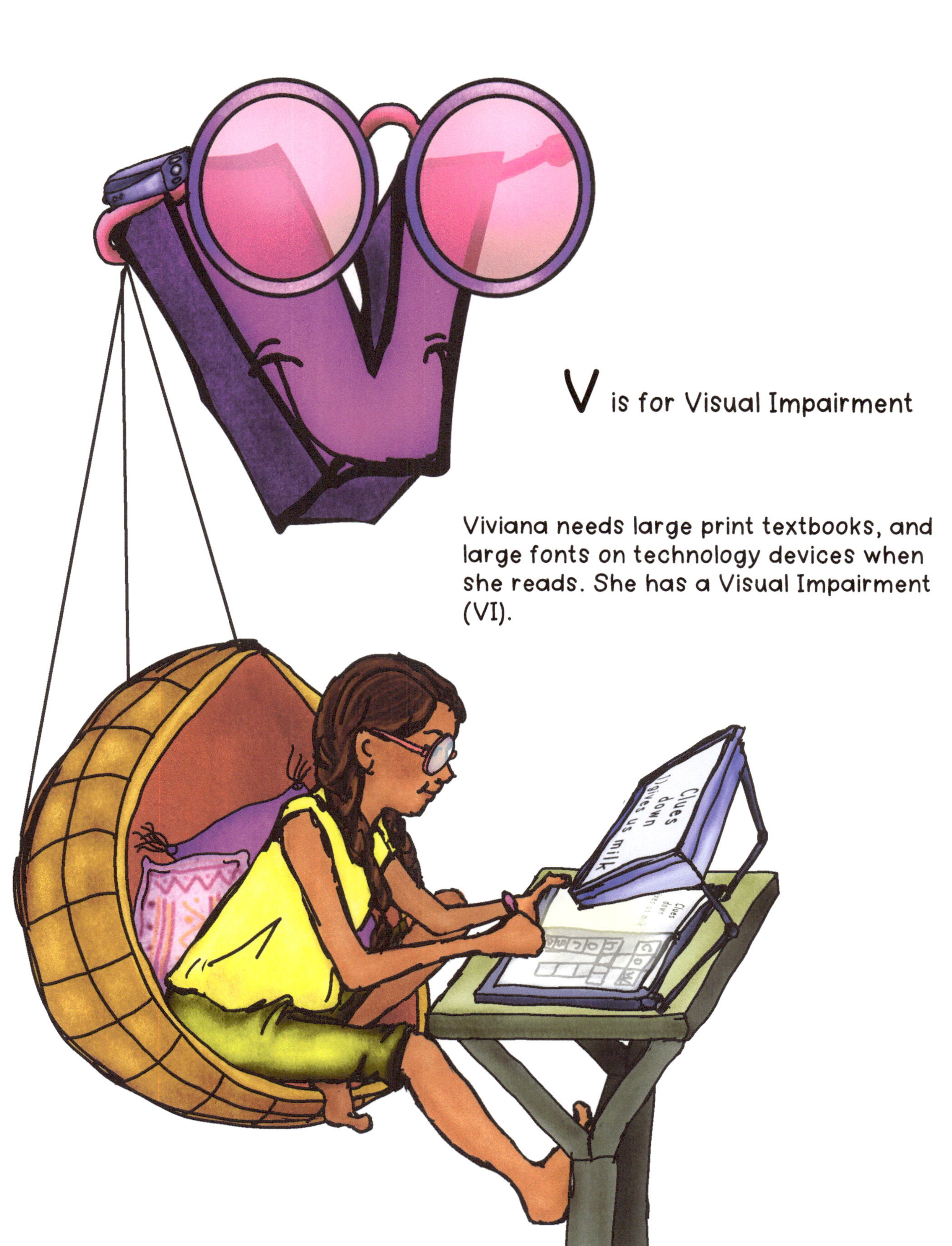

V is for Visual Impairment

Viviana needs large print textbooks, and large fonts on technology devices when she reads. She has a Visual Impairment (VI).

At school, Willie plays adaptive sports in Adaptive PE class, in his sports wheelchair. Disabled athletes can use an electric or a manual wheelchair.

 is for Fragile X Syndrome

Fragile X Syndrome is a gene mutation on the X chromosome that can affect boys and girls. Sometimes the syndrome can create unusual physical traits such as a large forehead with large ears that stick out. Possible mild to severe intellectual disabilities can also exist along with Autistic like behaviors. Think of the Fragile X Chromosome like a worn and torn pair of jeans.

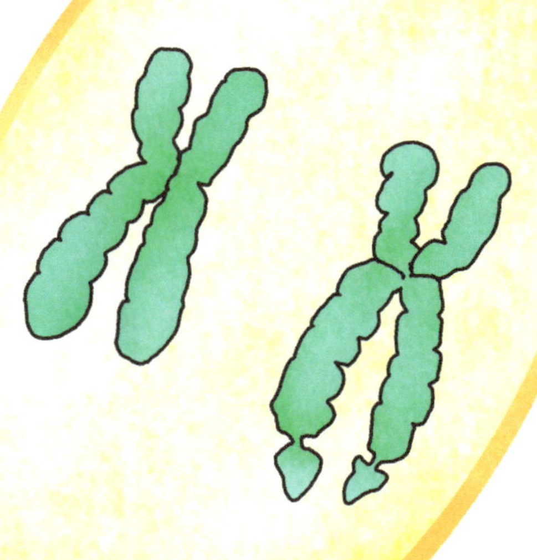

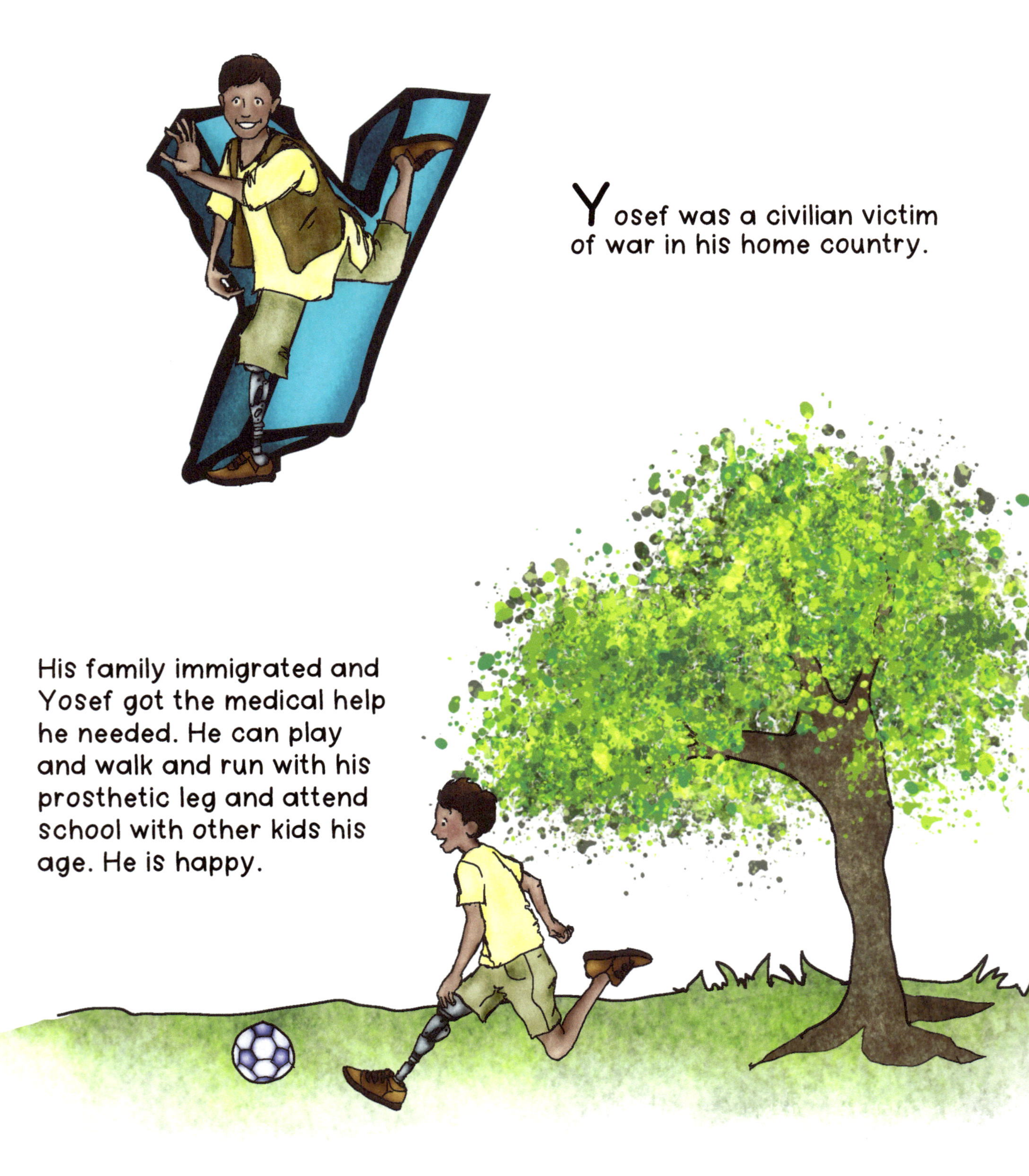

Yosef was a civilian victim of war in his home country.

His family immigrated and Yosef got the medical help he needed. He can play and walk and run with his prosthetic leg and attend school with other kids his age. He is happy.

Z is for The Zeus Patrol:

Join The Zeus Patrol!
Membership and dues are free!
Wear your shield as your badge of courage!

The Greek shield with the lightning bolt symbolizes confidence and courage. The lightning bolt gives you the courage to speak up when someone who looks, acts, or thinks differently than you, becomes a victim of bullying. Confidence to be a friend to someone who is disabled is a form of kindness. Offering a helping hand can make you feel good.

Resources

The Webster Dictionary definition of disability is: "a physical, mental, cognitive, or developmental condition that impairs, interferes with, or limits a person's ability to engage in certain tasks or actions or participate in typical daily activities and interactions." The Merriam-Webster Dictionary, New Edition, 2022 Copyright, Mass-Market Paperback – Softcover.

The Americans With Disabilities Act (ADA) defines a person with a disability as "…a person who has a physical or mental impairment that substantially limits one or more major life activity." Americans With Disabilities Act of 1990, 42 U.S.C. § 12101 et seq. (1990)

The Americans with Disabilities Act of 1990 (ADA) and subsequent ADA Amendments Act of 2008 (ADAAA) define a "major life activity" as including, but not limited to, "caring for oneself, performing manual tasks, seeing, hearing, eating, sleeping, walking, standing, lifting, bending, speaking, breathing, learning, ..." ADA Amendments Act of 2008, Pub. L, No. 110-325 (2008), https://govinfo.gov/app/details/PLAW-110publ325.

The following Special Education Laws can be found at: U.S. Department of Education https://ed.gov.

Brown vs The Board of Education (1954)

Rehabilitation Act of 1973 (Section 504 Plans)

Public Law 94-142, Education for All Handicapped Children Act (EHA) (1975)

Individuals with Disabilities Education Act (IDEA) (1990)

Americans with Disabilities Act (1990)

No Child Left Behind (2001)

List of IEP Eligibilities from the Individuals with Disabilities Education Act (IDEA):

Autism Spectrum Disorder
Deaf
Deaf and Blind
Emotional Disturbance
Hearing Impairment
Intellectual Disability
Multiple Disabilities
Orthopedic Impairment
Other Health Impairment
Specific Learning Disability
Speech and Language Impairment
Traumatic Brain Injury
Visual Impairment

California Department of Education, Program Guidelines For Individuals Who Are Severely Orthopedically Impaired, CA Department of Education, 1992.

Origins of the word 'Handicap':

Baynton, Douglas. "Language Matters: Handicapping an Affliction." Disability History Museum, https://disabilityhistorymuseum.org. Accessed 15 January 2024.

Mikkelson, Barbara. "Etymology of Handicap." Snopes, https://snopes.com. Accessed 15 January 2024

Lawrence M. Siegel is a Special Education attorney and advocate who has published a number of informative books.

Siegel, Lawrence. The Complete IEP Guide, How to Advocate for Special Education Services for Your Child, 11th edition, Copyright 2023, Nolo, 2023. https://nolo.com.

Resources (continued)

"National Center for Advancing of Translational Sciences." Rare Diseases, GARD Genetic and Rare Diseases Information Center, 2024, https://rarediseases.info.nih.gov.

"We Have A Beautiful and Rare Chance." National Organization of Rare Disorders, NORD, 2024, https://rarediseases.org.

Harris, John. "The Mother of Neurodiversity: How Judy Singer Changed the World." The Guardian, September 5, 2023, https://theguardian.com. Accessed 10 Oct. 2023.

Singer, Judy. Neurodiversity: the birth of an idea, Judy Singer pub., 2017.

Odd People In: The Birth of Community Amongst People on The Autism Spectrum: A Personal Exploration of a New Social Movement Based on Neurological Diversity Singer J, (1998) An Honours Thesis presented to the Faculty of Humanities and Social Science, the University of Technology, Sydney, 1998.

United Disabilities Services, UDS Foundation, "Types of Service Dogs and How They Benefit People with Disabilities," February 15, 2020 https://udservices.org.

UNICEF Data "Children with Disabilities," unicef | for every child, June 2023, http://data.unicef.org.

About the Author

 One of Mary's brothers sustained Cerebral Palsy and deafness shortly after birth in the 1950's. This began her lifelong experience with the disabled.

Mary has a B.A. in Communications from UNC Greeley, Colorado and an M.A. in Educational Administration from CSUN Northridge, California. She also has a Secondary English Teaching Credential, a Language Development Specialist Certificate, a Special Education Credential: authorization (PHI) Physically Handicapped Impairment which covers Orthopedic and Other Health Impairments, as well as an Educational Administration Credential.

She began her career as a preschool teacher/director. Mary then taught in the Los Angeles Unified School District as a Special Ed. classroom teacher, telephone teacher, and hospital teacher. She went on to be an O.I. Itinerant and case manager until retiring in 2017. A combined 37 years in education.

Her husband is also an LAUSD high school educator and music teacher. They have a grown-up daughter who has a Siberian Husky they frequently dog sit.

About the Illustrator

It was a pleasure for Sarah and 'The Pen' to join Mary Kaluza-Maxson in her clever, and knowledgeable, ABCD book showcasing the wonderful adaptive equipment available to help people deal with their life challenges.

Sarah Gledhill lives in Lancashire, United Kingdom.

After decades spent bouncing around the hot African veld in a Landy, sharing life and adventures with four sons and a wonderful variety of animals, Sarah is now happily rediscovering the cherished, fragile worlds of the hedgerows, woodlands, waterways and dry stone walls of the UK.

About Atmosphere Press

Atmosphere Press is an independent, full-service publisher for excellent books in all genres and for all audiences. Learn more about what we do at atmospherepress.com.

We encourage you to check out some of Atmosphere's latest releases, which are available at Amazon.com and via order from your local bookstore:

Alley: I Have Albinism, by Alethea Allen
Santa on a Surfboard, by Laura Sharp
Lilah Loves Life, by Brian Sullivan
The Christmas Witch, by Jaime Katusha
My Sister is Sick . . . What About Me?, by Mary Kay and Eli Olson
There's a Spider in My Bed, by Devon Nunnally and Biaina Alexanian
Yikes, I Saw a Barracuda!, by Tamara Anderson
Winston's Big Wind, by Barbara Reyelts
Holidays in Trees: Harvest Festival, by Cammy Marble
The Tail of a Trio, by Katherine Scott
Cow Days, by Christina Warfel
Logan and Lexi Meditate, by Denesia D. Rogers
It's Just a Heart, by Kathy Kay